John Kember and Martin Beech

Guitar Sight-Reading 1

Déchiffrage pour la guitare 1
Vom-Blatt-Spiel auf der Gitarre 1

A fresh approach / Nouvelle approche
Eine erfrischend neue Methode

ED 12955
ISMN M-2201-2568-3
ISBN 978-1-902455-78-5

www.schott-music.com

Mainz · London · Madrid · New York · Paris · Prague · Tokyo · Toronto
© 2007 SCHOTT MUSIC Ltd, London · Printed in Germany

ED 12955

British Library Cataloguing-in-Publication Data.
A catalogue record for this book is available from the British Library
ISMN M-2201-2568-3
ISBN 978-1-902455-78-5

© 2007 Schott Music Ltd, London.

French translation: Agnès Ausseur
German translation: Uta Pastowski
Cover design by www.adamhaystudio.com
Music setting and page layout by Jackie Leigh
Printed in Germany S&Co.8212

Contents
Sommaire / Inhalt

Preface

Guitar Sight-Reading 1 aims to establish good practice and provide an early introduction to the essential skill of sight-reading.

Ideally, sight-reading should be a regular part of a student's routine each time they play the guitar, both in the practice room and in a lesson.

This book aims to establish the habit early in a student's guitar playing. Of course, names of notes and time values need to be thoroughly known and understood but sight-reading is equally helped by an awareness of shape and direction.

There are six sections in this book, each of which introduces new notes, rhythms, dynamics and Italian terms in a logical sequence, much as you would find in a beginner's tutor book. The emphasis is on providing idiomatic tunes and structures rather than sterile sight-reading exercises. Each section begins with several solo examples and concludes with duets and accompanied pieces, enabling the player to gain experience of sight-reading within the context of ensemble playing. In the accompanied pieces, the choice of both piano and guitar accompaniments are provided together with chord indications.

Section 1 uses the three open treble strings G, B and E, together with simple rhythms in 4-time.

Section 2 continues to use the three treble strings and extends the range from G to G in first position. Movement is mainly by step and 3-time is introduced together with the dotted minim.

Section 3 stays with the treble strings but adds the open bass strings E, A and D.

Section 4 introduces first position on the bass strings, 2-time and quavers in pairs.

Section 5 introduces the key signatures of G major and E minor, and the new notes F♯, C♯ and D♯. Treble melodies with open bass strings are continued with the addition of use of ♩. ♪ rhythms in 2-, 3- and 4-time. Simple dynamic markings are introduced, as are performance directions.

Section 6 completes this first book with more complex examples in the above times, with the addition of F major and D minor, and notes B♭ and G♯.

To the pupil: why sight-reading?

When you are faced with a new piece and asked to play it, whether at home, in a lesson, or in an exam or audition, there is no one there to help you – except yourself! Sight-reading tests your ability to read the time and notes correctly, and to observe the phrasing and dynamics quickly.

The aim of this book is to help you to teach yourself. The book gives guidance on what to look for and how best to prepare in a very short time by observing the time and key signatures, the shape of the melody, and marks of expression. These short pieces progress gradually to help you to build up your confidence and observation, and enable you to sight-read accurately. At the end of each section there are duets to play with your teacher or friends, and pieces with accompaniment – on either piano or guitar – which will test your ability to sight-read while something else is going on. This is a necessary skill when playing with a band or accompanying singers.

If you sight-read something every time you play your guitar, you will be amazed at how much better you will become. Remember: if you can sight-read most of the tunes you are asked to learn, you will be able to concentrate on the 'tricky bits' and complete them quickly.

Think of the tunes in this book as mini-pieces, and try to learn them quickly and correctly. Then when you are faced with real sight-reading, you will be well-equipped to succeed at the first attempt.

You are on your own now!

Préface

Le propos de ce premier volume de déchiffrage pour la guitare est de fournir une initiation et un entraînement solide aux principes de la lecture à vue.

L'idéal serait que le déchiffrage prenne régulièrement place dans la routine de travail de l'élève à chaque fois qu'il prend sa guitare, chez lui ou pendant la leçon.

L'objectif est ici d'établir l'habitude de la lecture à vue très tôt dans l'étude de la guitare. Le déchiffrage suppose, bien sûr, que les noms et les valeurs de notes soient complètement assimilés et compris mais il s'appuie également sur la reconnaissance des contours et de la direction mélodique.

Ce volume comporte six parties dont chacune correspond à l'introduction de notes, de rythmes, de nuances dynamiques et de termes italiens nouveaux selon la progression logique rencontrée dans une méthode de guitare pour débutant. La démarche consiste à fournir des airs et des structures propres au répertoire de la guitare de préférence à de stériles exercices de déchiffrage. Chaque partie débute par plusieurs pièces en solo et se termine par des duos et des pièces accompagnées de manière à familiariser l'instrumentiste avec le déchiffrage collectif. L'accompagnement est proposé au choix au piano ou à la guitare pour les pièces accompagnées, ainsi que les indications d'accords.

Section 1 – Les trois cordes supérieures à vide de *sol, si* et *mi* et rythmes simples à 4 temps.

Section 2 – Les trois cordes supérieures à vide et extension de la tessiture de *sol* à *sol* en première position. Mouvements mélodiques principalement conjoints et introduction de la mesure à 3 temps et de la blanche pointée.

Section 3 – Toujours sur les trois cordes supérieures. Introduction des cordes à vide inférieures *mi, la* et *ré*.

Section 4 – Introduction de la première position sur les cordes graves, de la mesure à 2 temps et des croches par deux.

Section 5 – Introduction de l'armure des tonalités de *sol* majeur et de *mi* mineur, des nouvelles notes *fa*♯, *do*♯ et *ré*♯. Mélodies dans l'aigu avec cordes graves à vide. Introduction du rythme ♩. ♪ dans des mesures à 2, 3 et 4 temps. Introduction de nuances dynamiques simples et d'indications d'expression.

Section 6 – Conclusion de ce premier volume par l'introduction d'exemples plus complexes des mesures précédentes et introduction des tonalités de *fa* majeur et de *ré* mineur et des notes *si*♭ et *sol*♯.

A l'élève : Pourquoi le déchiffrage ?

Lorsque vous vous trouvez face à un nouveau morceau que l'on vous demande de jouer, que ce soit chez vous, pendant une leçon ou lors d'un examen ou d'une audition, personne d'autre ne peut vous aider que vous-même ! Le déchiffrage met à l'épreuve votre capacité à lire correctement les rythmes et les notes et à saisir rapidement le phrasé et les nuances.

Ce recueil se propose de vous aider à vous entraîner vous-même. Il vous oriente sur ce que vous devez repérer et sur la meilleure manière de vous préparer en un laps de temps très court en sachant observer les indications de mesure et l'armure à la clef de la tonalité, les contours de la mélodie et les indications expressives. Ces pièces brèves, en progressant par étapes, vous feront prendre de l'assurance, aiguiseront vos observations et vous permettront de lire à vue avec exactitude et aisance. A la fin de chaque partie figurent des duos que vous pourrez jouer avec votre professeur ou des amis et des morceaux avec accompagnement – soit au piano, soit à la guitare – qui mettront à l'épreuve votre habileté à déchiffrer pendant que se déroule une autre partie. Celle-ci est indispensable pour jouer avec un ensemble ou pour accompagner des chanteurs.

Vous serez surpris de vos progrès si vous déchiffrez une pièce à chaque fois que vous vous mettez à la guitare. N'oubliez pas que si vous êtes capable de lire à vue la plupart des morceaux que vous allez étudier, vous pourrez vous concentrer sur les passages difficiles et les assimiler plus vite.

Considérez ces pages comme des « mini-morceaux » et essayez de les apprendre rapidement et sans erreur de manière à ce que, devant un véritable déchiffrage, vous soyez bien armé pour réussir dès la première lecture.

A vous seul de jouer maintenant !

Vorwort

Vom-Blatt-Spiel auf der Gitarre 1 möchte zu einer guten Übetechnik verhelfen und frühzeitig für die Einführung der grundlegenden Fähigkeiten des Vom-Blatt-Spiels sorgen.

Das Vom-Blatt-Spiel sollte idealerweise ein regelmäßiger Bestandteil des Gitarrenspiels werden, sowohl beim Üben als auch im Unterricht.

Die vorliegende Ausgabe hat das Ziel, diese Gewohnheit beim Schüler bereits von Anfang an zu verankern. Natürlich muss man dazu die Notennamen und Notenwerte kennen und verstanden haben; außerdem ist das Bewusstsein für Form und Richtung eine wichtige Grundlage für das Vom-Blatt-Spiel.

Diese Ausgabe besteht aus sechs Teilen, in denen nach und nach neue Noten, Rhythmen, Artikulationen, dynamische Angaben und italienische Begriffe in einer logischen Abfolge eingeführt werden, ganz ähnlich wie in einer Schule für Anfänger. Der Schwerpunkt liegt mehr auf der Bereitstellung passender Melodien und Strukturen als auf abstrakten Vom-Blatt-Spiel-Übungen. In jedem Teil findet man zuerst einige Solobeispiele und anschließend Duette und begleitete Stücke, damit man auch beim Zusammenspiel mit anderen Erfahrungen im Vom-Blatt-Spiel sammeln kann. Bei den begleiteten Stücken werden sowohl Klavier- als auch Gitarrenbegleitungen sowie Akkordangaben zur Verfügung gestellt.

Teil 1 verwendet die drei leeren Diskantsaiten G, H und E sowie einfache Rhythmen im 4/4-Takt.

Teil 2 verwendet weiterhin die drei Diskantsaiten, und der Tonumfang in der 1. Lage wird von G bis G erweitert. Die Bewegungen finden hauptsächlich schrittweise statt, und der 3/4-Takt wird zusammen mit der punktierten halben Note eingeführt.

Teil 3 verweilt bei den Diskantsaiten, es kommen aber die leeren Basssaiten E, A und D hinzu.

Teil 4 führt die 1. Lage auf den Basssaiten, den 2/4-Takt und Achtelnoten ein.

Teil 5 führt die Tonarten G-Dur und e-Moll sowie die neuen Noten Fis, Cis und Dis ein. Es werden weiterhin die Diskantsaiten und leere Basssaiten verwendet, jedoch mit der Ergänzung von Rhythmen ♩. ♪ im 2/4-, 3/4- und 4/4-Takt. Es werden außerdem einfache dynamische Angaben und Vortragsbezeichnungen eingeführt.

Teil 6 beendet diesen ersten Band mit komplexeren Beispielen in den oben erwähnten Taktarten. Es kommen außerdem die Tonarten F-Dur und d-Moll sowie die Noten B und Gis hinzu.

An den Schüler: Warum Vom-Blatt-Spiel?

Wenn du mit einem neuen Musikstück konfrontiert wirst und man dich bittet, es zu spielen – ob zu Hause, im Unterricht, in einer Prüfung oder in einem Vorspiel –, gibt es niemanden, der dir dabei helfen kann – nur du selbst! Das Vom-Blatt-Spiel überprüft deine Fähigkeit, die Taktart und die Noten richtig zu lesen sowie Phrasierungen und dynamische Angaben schnell zu erfassen.

Ziel der vorliegenden Ausgabe ist es, dich beim Selbstunterricht zu unterstützen. Die Ausgabe zeigt dir, worauf man beim Vom-Blatt-Spiel achten sollte und wie man sich innerhalb kurzer Zeit am besten vorbereitet, indem man sich die Takt- und Tonarten, den Verlauf der Melodie und die Vortragsbezeichnungen genau ansieht. Die kurzen Musikstücke steigern sich vom Schwierigkeitsgrad her allmählich, um dein Selbstvertrauen und deine Beobachtungsgabe zu fördern und um dich zum exakten Vom-Blatt-Spiel zu befähigen. Am Ende eines jeden Teils finden sich Duette, die du mit deinem Lehrer oder deinen Freunden zusammen spielen kannst, sowie Stücke mit Begleitung – entweder mit Klavier oder mit Gitarre. Sie sollen deine Fähigkeit überprüfen, ein Stück vom Blatt zu spielen, während gleichzeitig etwas anderes passiert. Das ist eine wichtige Grundlage für das Zusammenspiel mit einer Band oder wenn man einen Sänger begleiten möchte.

Wenn du beim Gitarre spielen jedes Mal auch ein Stück vom Blatt spielst, wirst du bald merken, wie du immer besser wirst. Denk daran: Wenn du die Melodien, die du spielen sollst, vom Blatt spielen kannst, kannst du dich auf die „komplizierten Dinge" konzentrieren und diese viel schneller erlernen.

Stelle dir die Melodien in dieser Ausgabe als kleine Stücke vor und versuche, sie möglichst schnell und korrekt zu erlernen. Wenn du dann wirklich ein Stück vom Blatt spielen musst, wirst du bestens vorbereitet sein, um gleich beim ersten Versuch erfolgreich zu sein.

Jetzt bist du auf dich selbst gestellt!

Section 1 – Open treble strings
Section 1 – Cordes supérieures à vide
Teil 1 – Leere Diskantsaiten

Three steps to success

1. **Look at the top number of the time signature**. It shows the number of beats in a bar. Tap (or clap, sing or play one note) the rhythm, feeling the pulse throughout. Count at least one bar of the time signature in your head to set up the pulse before you begin to tap or play.

2. **Look for patterns**. While tapping the rhythm, look at the melodic shape and notice movement by step, skip, repeated notes and sequences (short, repeated melodic phrases which often rise or fall by step).

3. **Keep going**. Remember: a wrong note or rhythm can be corrected the next time you play it. If you stop, you have doubled the mistake!

Trois étapes vers la réussite

1. **Observez le chiffre supérieur de l'indication de mesure**. Il indique le nombre de pulsations contenues par mesure. Frappez (dans les mains, chantez ou jouez sur une seule note) le rythme tout en maintenant une pulsation intérieure constante. Comptez mentalement au moins une mesure complète pour installer la pulsation avant de frapper ou de jouer chaque pièce.

2. **Repérez les motifs**. Tout en frappant le rythme, observez les contours de la mélodie et relevez les mouvements par degrés, les sauts d'intervalles, les notes répétées et les séquences (courtes phrases mélodiques répétées progressant généralement par degrés ascendants ou descendants).

3. **Ne vous arrêtez pas**. Vous pourrez corriger une fausse note ou un rythme inexact la prochaine fois que vous jouerez. En vous interrompant, vous doublez la faute !

Drei Schritte zum Erfolg

1. **Sieh dir die obere Zahl der Taktangabe an**. Diese zeigt die Anzahl der Schläge in einem Takt an. Schlage (klatsche, singe oder spiele eine Note) den Rhythmus, wobei du immer das Metrum spüren solltest. Zähle mindestens einen Takt lang die Taktangabe im Kopf vor, um das Metrum zu verinnerlichen, bevor du zu spielen oder schlagen beginnst.

2. **Achte auch auf Muster**. Sieh dir die melodische Form an, während du den Rhythmus schlägst, und achte auf Bewegungen in Schritten oder Sprüngen sowie auf sich wiederholende Noten und Sequenzen (kurze, sich wiederholende melodische Phrasen, die oft schrittweise ansteigen oder abfallen).

3. **Spiele immer weiter**. Denk daran: Eine falsche Note oder ein falscher Rhythmus kann beim nächsten Mal korrigiert werden. Wenn du aber aufhörst zu spielen, verdoppelst du den Fehler!

Section 1 – Open treble strings
Section 1 – Cordes supérieures à vide
Teil 1 – Leere Diskantsaiten

2nd string.   2ème corde.   2. Saite.

3rd string.   3ème corde.   3. Saite.

1st and 2nd strings.   1ère et 2ème cordes.   1. und 2. Saite.

10

15.

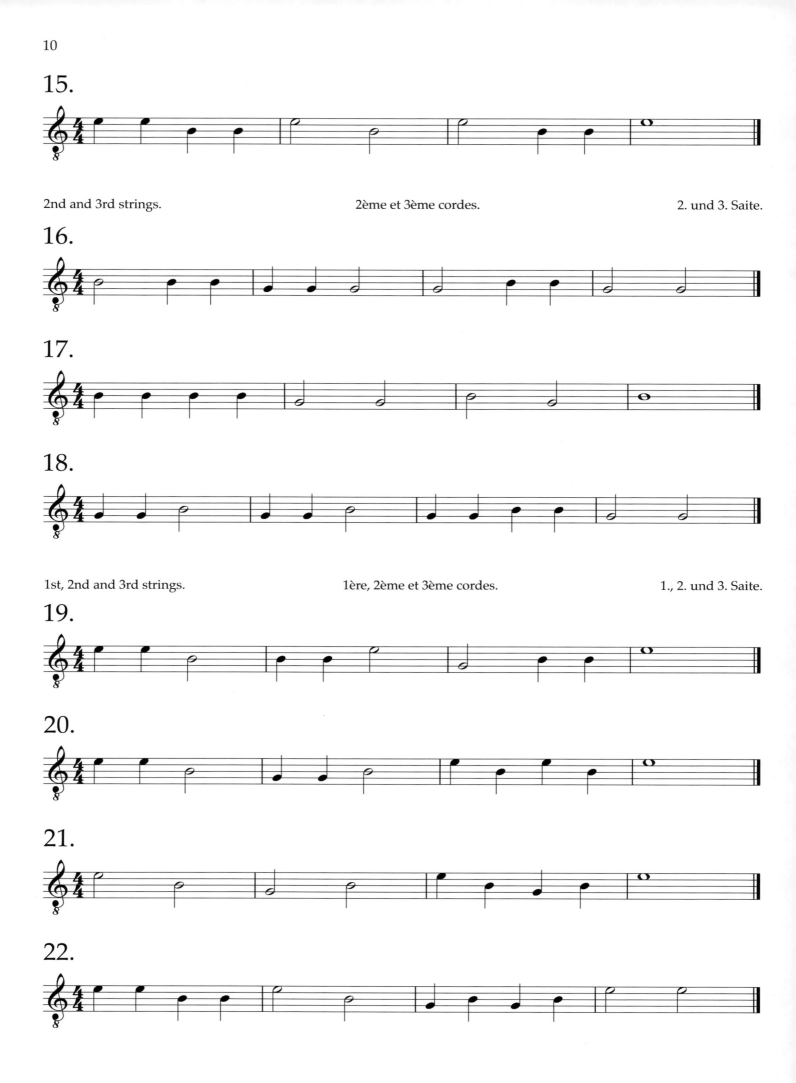

2nd and 3rd strings.　　　　　　　2ème et 3ème cordes.　　　　　　　2. und 3. Saite.

16.

17.

18.

1st, 2nd and 3rd strings.　　　　1ère, 2ème et 3ème cordes.　　　　1., 2. und 3. Saite.

19.

20.

21.

22.

23.

24.

25.

26.

27.

28.

Pupil / Elève / Schüler

Teacher / Professeur / Lehrer

29.

30.

31.

32.

33.

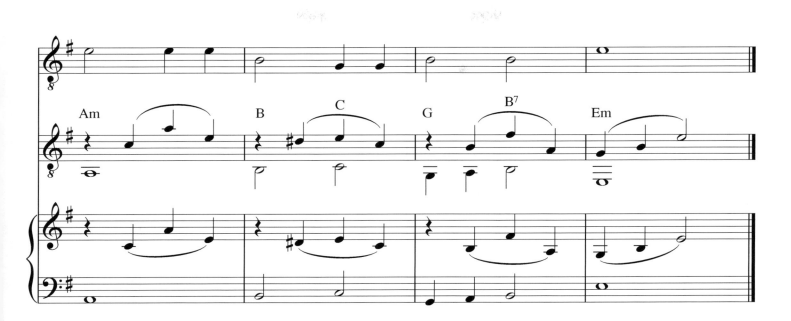

34.

Section 2 – Treble-string notes in first position
Section 2 – Notes des cordes supérieures en première position
Teil 2 – Noten auf den Diskantsaiten in der 1. Lage

Four steps to success

1. **Look at the top number of the time signature**. It shows the number of beats in a bar. Tap (or clap, sing or play on one note) the rhythm, feeling the pulse throughout. Count at least one bar of the time signature in your head to set up the pulse before you begin to tap or play.

2. **Look for patterns**. While tapping the rhythm, look at the melodic shape and notice movement by step, skip, repeated notes and sequences (short, repeated melodic phrases that usually rise or fall by step).

3. **Spot the new notes** and make sure that you know their names.

4. **Keep going**. Remember: a wrong note or rhythm can be corrected the next time you play it. If you stop, you have doubled the mistake!

Quatre étapes vers la réussite

1. **Observez le chiffre supérieur de l'indication de mesure**. Il indique le nombre de pulsations contenues par mesure. Frappez (dans les mains, chantez ou jouez sur une seule note) le rythme tout en maintenant une pulsation intérieure constante. Comptez mentalement au moins une mesure pour installer la pulsation avant de frapper ou de jouer chaque pièce.

2. **Repérez les motifs**. Tout en frappant le rythme, observez les contours de la mélodie et relevez les mouvements par degrés, les sauts d'intervalles, les notes répétées ou les séquences.

3. **Repérez les nouvelles notes** et assurez-vous d'en connaître le nom.

4. **Ne vous arrêtez pas**. Vous pourrez corriger une fausse note ou un rythme inexact la prochaine fois que vous jouerez. En vous interrompant, vous doublez la faute !

Vier Schritte zum Erfolg

1. **Sieh dir die obere Zahl der Taktangabe an**. Diese zeigt die Anzahl der Schläge in einem Takt an. Schlage (klatsche, singe oder spiele eine Note) den Rhythmus, wobei du immer das Metrum spüren solltest. Zähle mindestens einen Takt lang die Taktangabe im Kopf vor, um das Metrum zu verinnerlichen, bevor du zu spielen oder schlagen beginnst.

2. **Achte auch auf Muster**. Sieh dir die melodische Form an, während du den Rhythmus schlägst, und achte auf Bewegungen in Schritten oder Sprüngen sowie auf sich wiederholende Noten und Sequenzen (kurze, sich wiederholende melodische Phrasen, die oft schrittweise ansteigen oder abfallen).

3. **Entdecke die neuen Noten** und vergewissere dich, dass du ihre Namen kennst.

4. **Spiele immer weiter**. Denk daran: Eine falsche Note oder ein falscher Rhythmus kann beim nächsten Mal korrigiert werden. Wenn du aber aufhörst zu spielen, verdoppelst du den Fehler!

Section 2 – Treble-string notes in first position

Section 2 – Notes des cordes supérieures en première position

Teil 2 – Noten auf den Diskantsaiten in der 1. Lage

1st string.   1ère corde.   1. Saite.

16

42.

43.

44.

45.

3rd string.   3ème corde.   3. Saite.

46.

47.

48.

49.

2nd and 3rd strings.   2ème et 3ème cordes.   2. und 3. Saite.

50.

17

51.

52.

53.

1st and 2nd strings.   1ère et 2ème cordes.   1. und 2. Saite.

54.

55.

56.

57.

Three treble strings.   Les cordes supérieures.   Drei Diskantsaiten.

58.

59.

60.

61.

62.

Introducing 3-time and
the dotted minim.
1st string.

Introduction de la mesure à 3 temps
et de la blanche pointée.
1ère corde.

Einführung des 3/4-Taktes und
der punktierten halben Note.
1. Saite.

63.

64.

2nd string.

2ème corde.

2. Saite.

65.

66.

19

2nd and 3rd strings.

2ème et 3ème cordes.

2. und 3. Saite.

67.

68.

Longer pieces using the three treble strings.

Pièces plus longues sur les cordes supérieures.

Längere Stücke auf den drei Diskantsaiten.

69.

70.

71.

Dotted minim in 4-time.

Blanche pointée dans une mesure à 4 temps.

Punktierte halbe Note im 4/4-Takt.

72.

73.

74.

20

75.

76.

77.

78.

79.

80.

81.

82.

83.

84.

85.

86.

87.

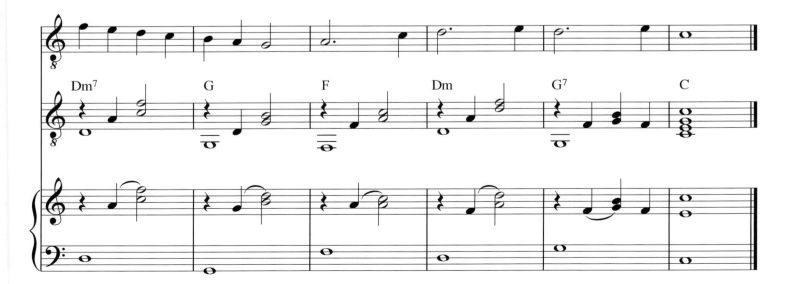

88.

89.

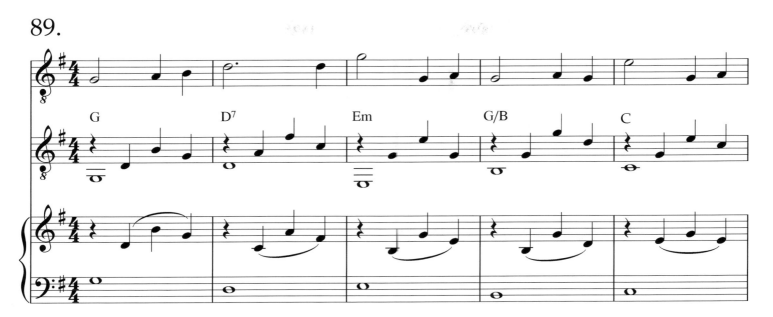

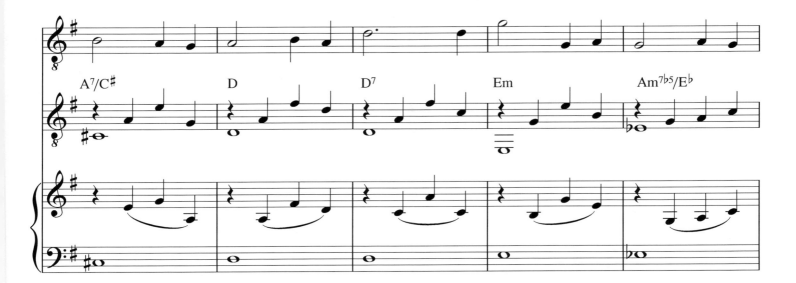

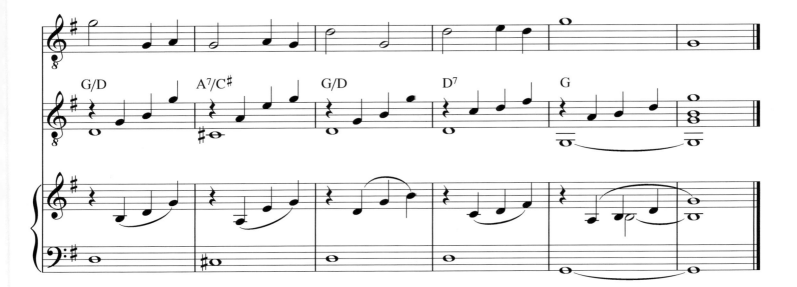

Section 3 – Treble notes with open bass strings
Section 3 – Notes aiguës avec cordes graves à vide
Teil 3 – Noten auf den Diskantsaiten und leere Basssaiten

Four steps to success

1. **Look at the top number of the time signature**. Tap (or clap, sing or play on one note) the rhythm, feeling the pulse throughout. Count at least one bar of the time signature in your head to set up the pulse before you begin to tap or play.

2. **Look for patterns**. While tapping the rhythm, look at the melodic shape and notice movement by step, skip, repeated notes or sequences.

3. **Look at the new bass notes** and make sure that you know which string to use.

4. **Keep going!**

Quatre étapes vers la réussite

1. **Observez le chiffre supérieur de l'indication de mesure**. Frappez (dans les mains, chantez ou jouez sur un seule note) le rythme tout en maintenant une pulsation intérieure constante. Comptez mentalement au moins une mesure pour installer la pulsation avant de frapper ou de jouer chaque pièce.

2. **Repérez les motifs**. Tout en frappant le rythme, observez les contours de la mélodie et repérez les déplacements par degrés, les sauts d'intervalles, les notes répétées et les séquences.

3. **Relevez les nouvelles notes de basse** et assurez-vous de savoir sur quelle corde les jouer.

4. **Ne vous arrêtez pas !**

Vier Schritte zum Erfolg

1. **Sieh dir die obere Zahl der Taktangabe an**. Schlage (klatsche, singe oder spiele eine Note) den Rhythmus, wobei du immer das Metrum spüren solltest. Zähle mindestens einen Takt lang die Taktangabe im Kopf vor, um das Metrum zu verinnerlichen, bevor du zu spielen oder schlagen beginnst.

2. **Achte auch auf Muster**. Sieh dir die melodische Form an, während du den Rhythmus schlägst, und achte auf Bewegungen in Schritten oder Sprüngen sowie auf sich wiederholende Noten und Sequenzen.

3. **Achte auf die neuen Bassnoten** und vergewissere dich, dass du weißt, welche Saite du verwenden musst.

4. **Spiele immer weiter!**

Section 3 – Treble notes with open bass strings
Section 3 – Notes aiguës avec cordes graves à vide
Teil 3 – Noten auf den Diskantsaiten und leere Basssaiten

1st string with
open bass strings.

1ère corde avec cordes
graves à vide.

1. Saite mit leeren
Basssaiten.

90.

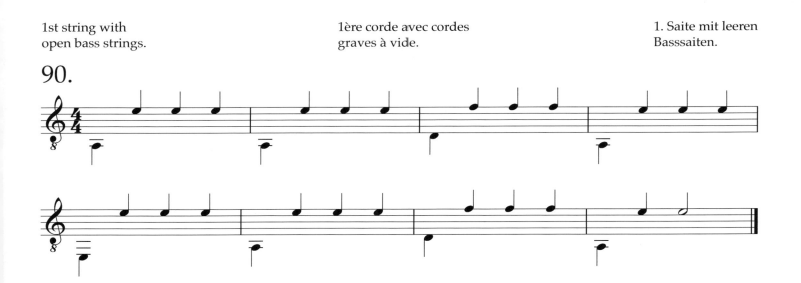

91.

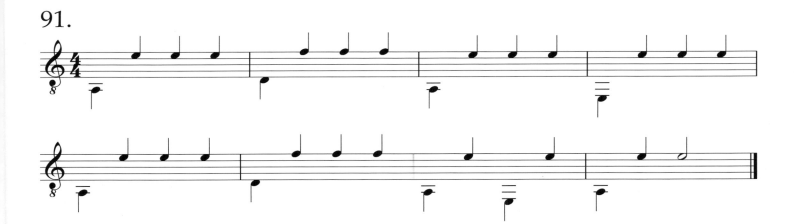

92.

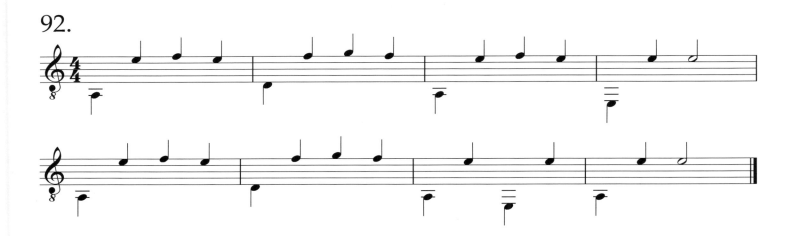

28

2nd string with
open bass strings.

2ème corde avec cordes
graves à vide.

2. Saite mit leeren
Basssaiten.

93.

94.

A and B with
open bass strings.

la et *si* avec cordes de
basse à vide.

A und B mit leeren
Basssaiten.

95.

96.

1st and 2nd strings with
open bass strings.

1ère et 2ème cordes avec
cordes graves à vide.

1. und 2. Saite mit
leeren Basssaiten.

97.

98.

99.

100.

101.

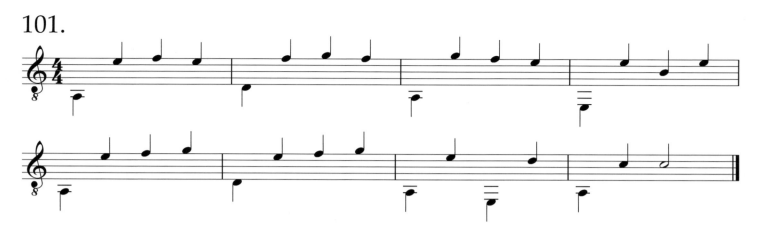

2nd and 3rd strings with open bass strings.

2ème et 3ème cordes avec cordes graves à vide.

2. und 3. Saite mit leeren Basssaiten.

102.

All three treble strings with open bass strings.

Les trois cordes supérieures avec cordes graves à vide.

Alle drei Diskantsaiten mit leeren Basssaiten.

103.

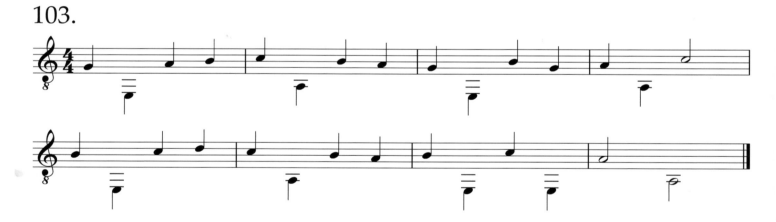

104.

105.

106.

107.

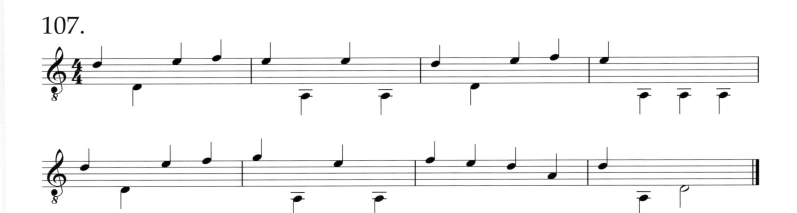

108.

109.

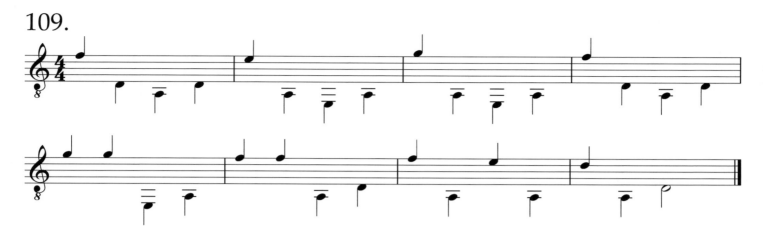

110.

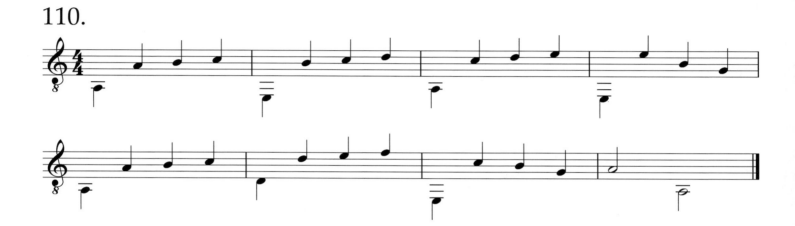

111.

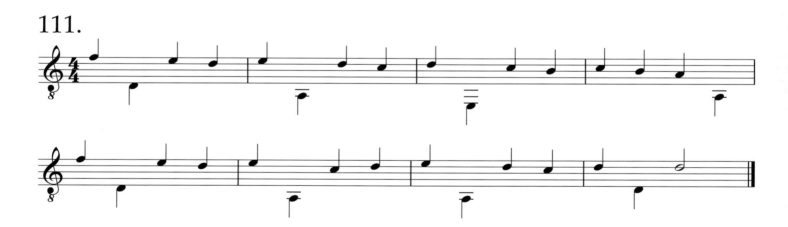

112.

113.

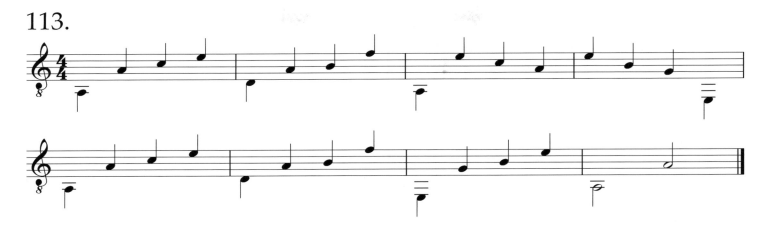

Note against note.   Note contre note.   Gleichzeitiger Anschlag der Töne.

114.

115.

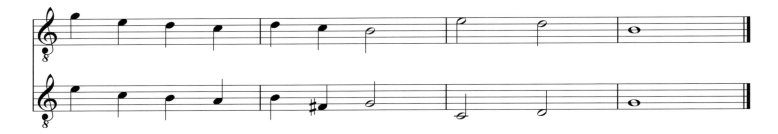

Independent rhythms.　　　　　　　　Rythmes indépendants.　　　　　　　　Unabhängige Rhythmen.

116.

117.

118.

119.

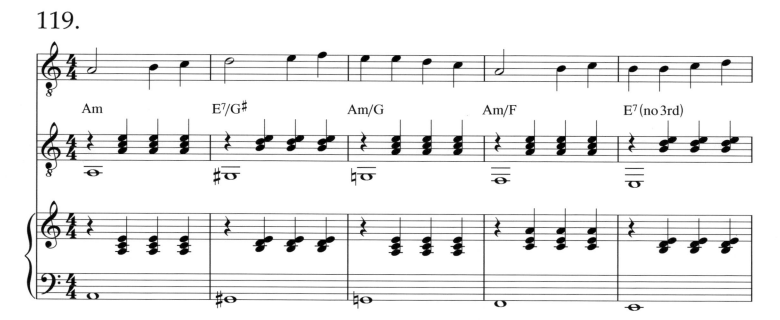

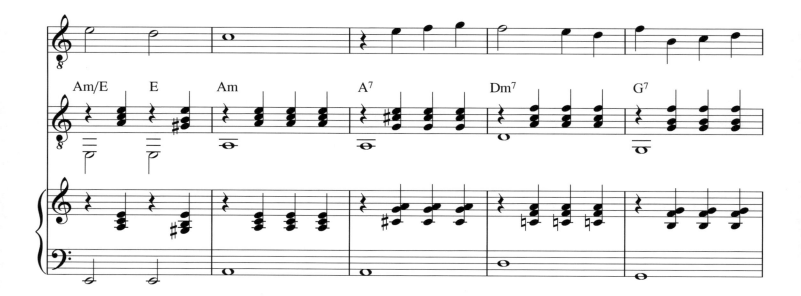

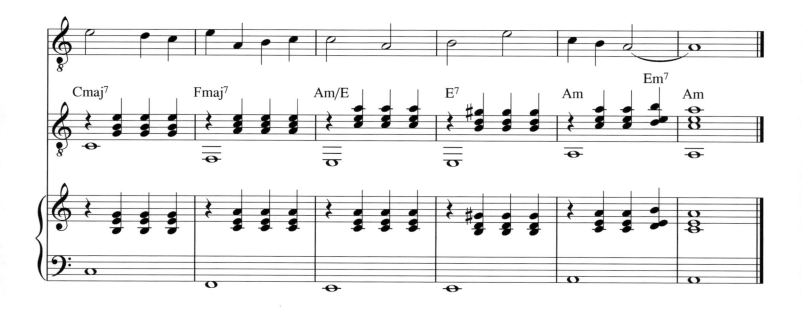

120.

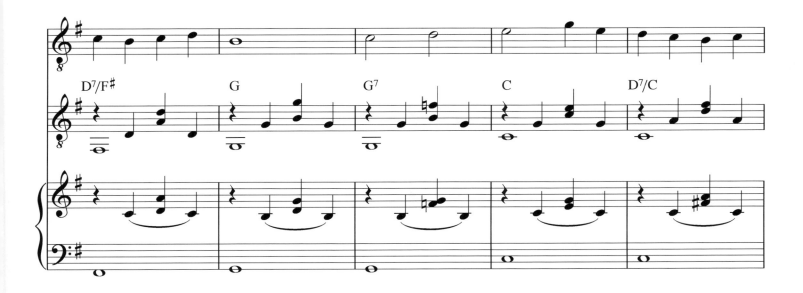

121.

Section 4 – First-position bass notes, quavers (eighth notes), dynamics and 2-time

Section 4 – Notes de basse en première position, croches, nuances dynamiques et mesure à 2 temps

Teil 4 – Noten auf den Basssaiten in der 1. Lage, Achtelnoten, dynamische Angaben und 2/4-Takt

Five steps to success

1. **Look at the top number of the time signature**. Tap (or clap, sing or play on one note) the rhythm, feeling the pulse throughout. Count at least one bar in your head to set up the pulse before you begin to tap or play.

2. **Look for patterns**. While tapping the rhythm, look at the melodic shape and notice movement by step, skip, repeated notes or sequences.

3. **Look at the new bass notes** and make sure that you know which string to use.

4. **Look for the new dynamic marks of** f (loud / strong) and p (quiet / gentle).

5. **Keep going!**

Cinq étapes vers la réussite

1. **Observez le chiffre supérieur de l'indication de mesure**. Frappez (dans les mains, chantez ou jouez sur un seule note) le rythme tout en maintenant une pulsation intérieure constante. Comptez mentalement au moins une mesure pour installer la pulsation avant de frapper ou de jouer chaque pièce.

2. **Repérez les motifs**. Tout en frappant le rythme, observez les contours de la mélodie et relevez les déplacements par degrés, les sauts d'intervalles, les notes répétées et les séquences.

3. **Relevez les nouvelles notes de basse** et assurez-vous de savoir sur quelle corde les jouer.

4. **Observez les nouvelles nuances dynamiques de** f (fort) et p (doux).

5. **Ne vous arrêtez pas !**

Fünf Schritte zum Erfolg

1. **Sieh dir die obere Zahl der Taktangabe an**. Schlage (klatsche, singe oder spiele eine Note) den Rhythmus, wobei du immer das Metrum spüren solltest. Zähle mindestens einen Takt im Kopf vor, um das Metrum zu verinnerlichen, bevor du zu spielen oder schlagen beginnst.

2. **Achte auch auf Muster**. Sieh dir die melodische Form an, während du den Rhythmus schlägst, und achte auf Bewegungen in Schritten oder Sprüngen sowie auf sich wiederholende Noten und Sequenzen.

3. **Achte auf die neuen Noten auf den Basssaiten** und vergewissere dich, dass du weißt, welche Saite du verwenden musst.

4. **Achte auf die neuen dynamischen Angaben** f (laut / kräftig) und p (leise / sanft).

5. **Spiele immer weiter!**

Section 4 – First-position bass notes, quavers (eighth notes), dynamics and 2-time

Section 4 – Notes de basse en première position, croches, nuances dynamiques et mesure à 2 temps

Teil 4 – Noten auf den Basssaiten in der 1. Lage, Achtelnoten, dynamische Angaben und 2/4-Takt

4th string.   4ème corde.   4. Saite.

4th string with quavers.   4ème corde avec croches.   4. Saite mit Achtelnoten.

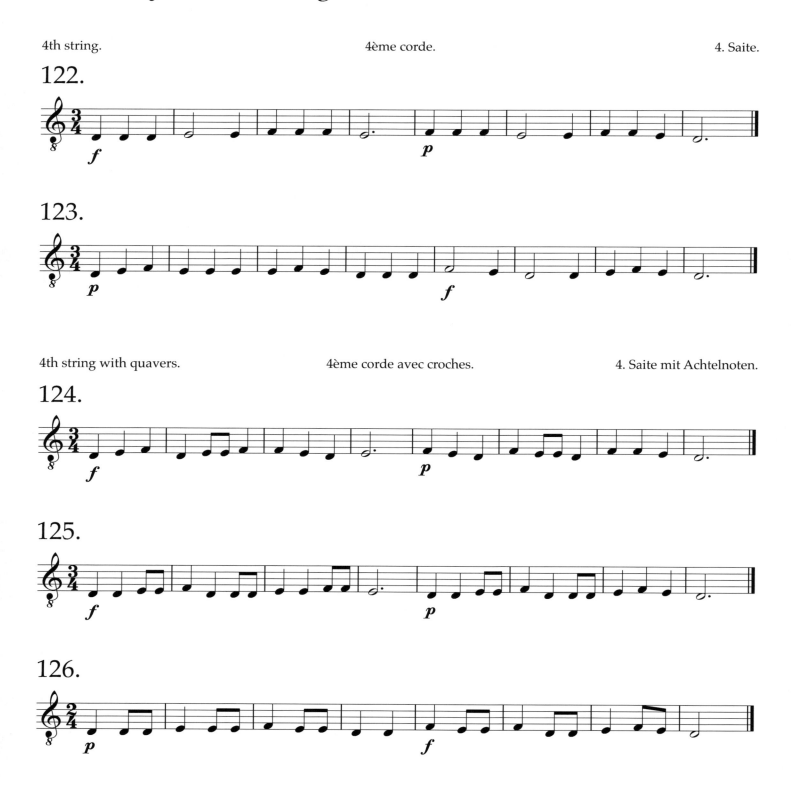

4th string with 5th open.   4ème corde avec 5ème corde à vide.   4. Saite mit leerer 5. Saite.

127.

128.

129.

5th string.   5ème corde.   5. Saite.

130.

131.

42

132.

133.
5th string with quavers.   5ème corde avec croches.   5. Saite mit Achtelnoten.

134.

4th and 5th strings.   4ème et 5ème cordes.   4. und 5. Saite.

135.

136.

137.

6th string.   6ème corde.   6. Saite.

138.

139.

5th and 6th strings.　　　　　5ème et 6ème cordes.　　　　　5. und 6. Saite.

140.

141.

Three bass strings.　　　　　Trois cordes graves.　　　　　Drei Basssaiten.

142.

143.

144.

44

145.

146.

147.

Three bass strings with quavers.   Trois cordes graves avec croches.   Drei Basssaiten mit Achtelnoten.

148.

149.

150.

4th string.   4ème corde.   4. Saite.

151.

4th string and open 5th.   4ème corde avec 5ème corde à vide.   4. Saite und leere 5. Saite.

152.

6th string.   6ème corde.   6. Saite.

153.

5th and 6th strings.   5ème et 6ème cordes.   5. und 6. Saite.

154.

155.

156.

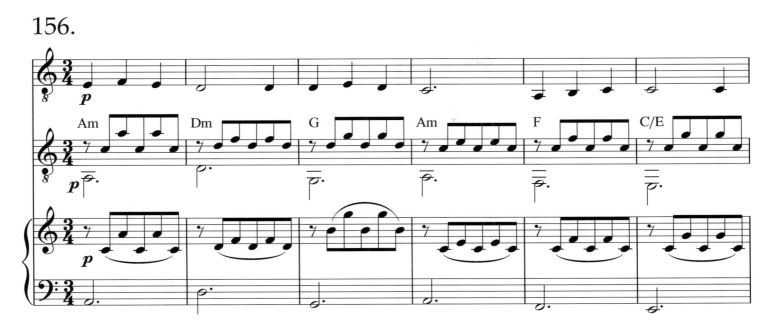

157.

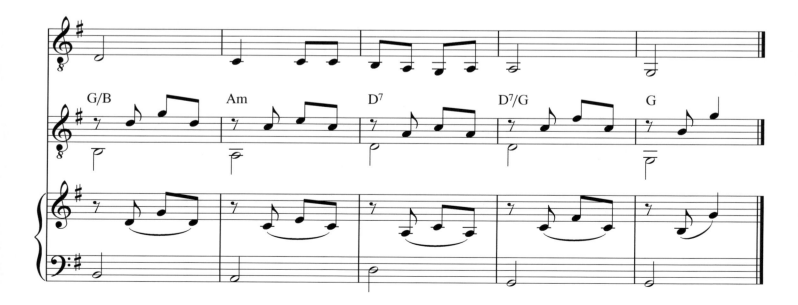

158.

Section 5 – New keys, dynamics and performance directions

Section 5 – Nouvelles tonalités, nuances dynamiques et indications d'expression

Teil 5 – Neue Tonarten, dynamische Angaben und Vortragsbezeichnungen

Five steps to success

1. **Look at the top number of the time signature**. Tap (or clap sing or play on one note) the rhythm, feeling the pulse throughout. Count at least one bar in your head before you begin to tap or play.

2. **Look for patterns and new rhythms**. While tapping the rhythm, look at the melodic shape, take note of the movement and see where the new bass notes fit the melody.

3. **Look between the treble clef and the time signature to see which sharps you need to remember**. Make sure you know which notes these apply to and look for additional sharps in the melody.

4. **Look for the dynamic marks** and observe the performance directions.

5. **Keep going!**

Terms and performance directions used in this section:
(You may note all directions and translations on the glossary page at the back of the book.)

Cinq étapes vers la réussite

1. **Observez le chiffre supérieur de l'indication de mesure**. Frappez (dans les mains, chantez ou jouez sur un seule note) le rythme tout en maintenant une pulsation intérieure constante. Comptez mentalement au moins une mesure pour installer la pulsation avant de frapper ou de jouer chaque pièce.

2. **Repérez les motifs**. Tout en frappant les rythmes, observez les contours de la mélodie notez le mouvement et repérez sous quelles notes de la mélodie se placent les notes de basse.

3. **Vérifiez les dièses placés entre la clé de *sol* et le chiffrage de la mesure**. Assurez-vous de savoir à quelles notes ils s'appliquent et repérez les altérations accidentelles dans le cours de la mélodie.

4. **Repérez les indications dynamiques** et respectez les indications d'expression.

5. **Ne vous arrêtez pas !**

Indications d'expression utilisées dans cette partie :
(Vous pourrez noter toutes les indications et leur traduction sur la page de glossaire en fin de volume.)

Fünf Schritte zum Erfolg

1. **Sieh dir die obere Zahl der Taktangabe an**. Schlage (klatsche, singe oder spiele eine Note) den Rhythmus, wobei du immer das Metrum spüren solltest. Zähle mindestens einen Takt im Kopf vor, um das Metrum zu verinnerlichen, bevor du zu spielen oder schlagen beginnst.

2. **Achte auch auf Muster und neue Rhythmen**. Sieh dir die melodische Form an, während du den Rhythmus schlägst, achte auf Bewegungen und erkenne, wo die neuen Bassnoten mit der Melodie zusammenpassen.

3. **Achte darauf, welche Vorzeichen zwischen dem Violinschlüssel und der Taktangabe stehen und merke sie dir gut**. Vergewissere dich, dass du weißt, zu welchen Noten diese Vorzeichen gehören und achte auf zusätzliche Vorzeichen im Verlauf des Stücks.

4. **Achte auf die dynamischen Angaben** und halte dich an die angegebenen Vortragsbezeichnungen.

5. **Spiele immer weiter!**

Vortragsbezeichnungen, die in diesem Teil vorkommen:
(Du kannst dir alle Angaben und ihre Übersetzungen in der Anhangseite hinten im Buch notieren.)

Adagio	slowly	lent	langsam
Andante	at a walking pace	allant	gehend
Con moto	with movement	avec mouvement	mit Bewegung
Leggiero	light	léger	leicht
Moderato	at a moderate speed	modéré	in gemäßigtem Tempo
Poco lento	a little slowly	un peu lent	etwas langsam

Section 5 – New keys, dynamics and performance directions

Section 5 – Nouvelles tonalités, nuances dynamiques et indications d'expression

Teil 5 – Neue Tonarten, dynamische Angaben und Vortragsbezeichnungen

First-position treble-string notes and open bass strings.

Notes de la première position de la corde mélodique avec cordes graves à vide.

Noten in der 1. Lage auf den Diskantsaiten und leere Basssaiten.

159.

160.

161.

162.

163.

First-position treble and
bass-string notes.

Notes de la corde mélodique et de
la corde grave en première position.

Noten auf den Diskant- und
Basssaiten in der 1. Lage.

164.

165.
Andante

166.
Moderato

167.
Con moto

168.
Moderato

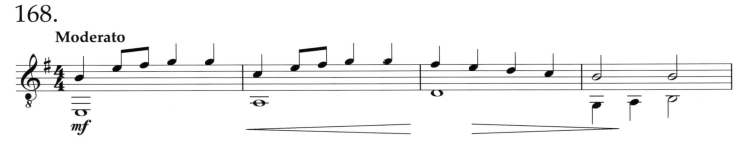

169.
Andante

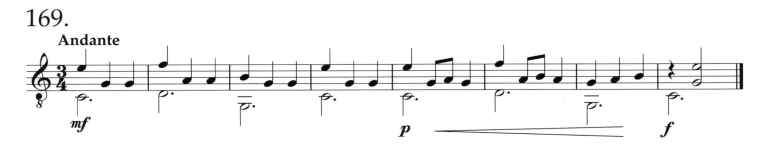

170.
Adagio

171.

172.

173.

174.

175.

176.

177.

178.

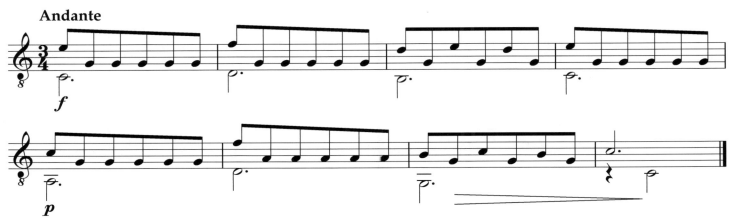

179.

180.

181.

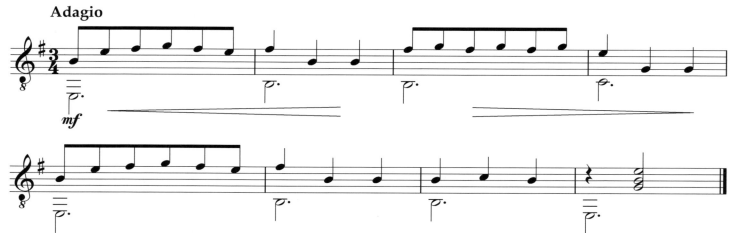

182.

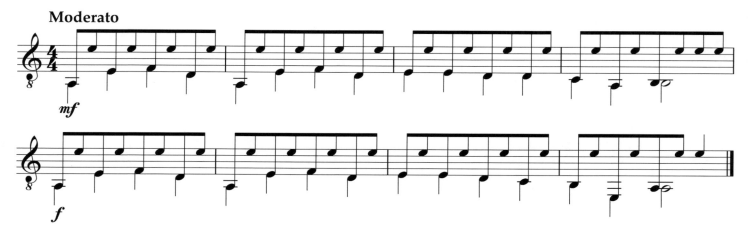

183.

184.

185.

186.

187.

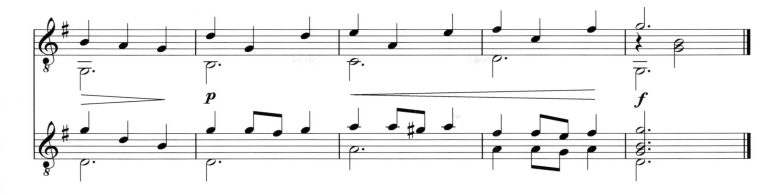

188.

189.

Con moto

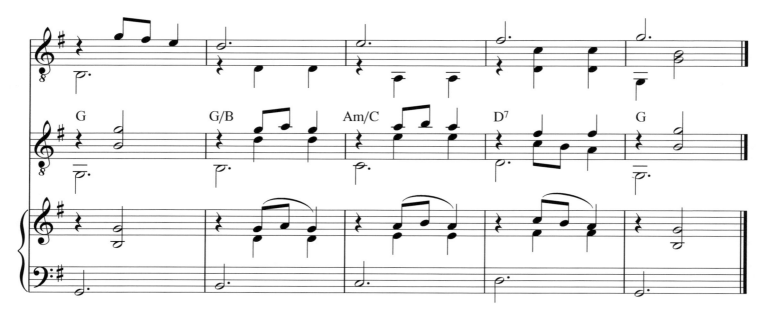

190.

191.

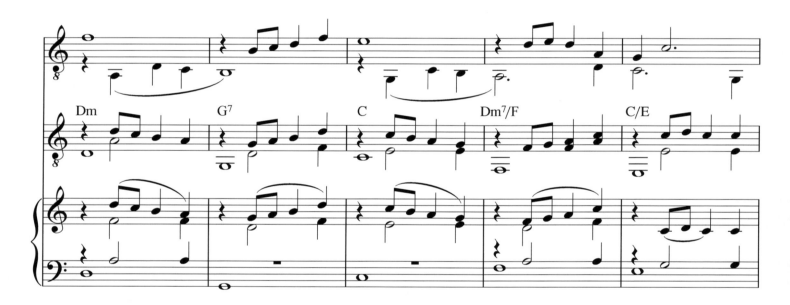

Section 6 – Revision; keys of F major and D minor
Section 6 – Révision ; tonalités de *fa* majeur et de *ré* mineur
Teil 6 – Durchsicht; die Tonarten F-Dur und d-Moll

Five steps to success

1. **Look at the top number of the time signature**. Tap (or clap, sing or play on one note) the rhythm, feeling the pulse throughout. Count at least one bar before you begin.

2. **Look for patterns**. While tapping the rhythm try to observe the shape, movement and style of the piece as indicated by the performance directions and dynamics.

3. **Look at the bass notes** and see where they occur and change.

4. **Look for any additional accidentals or instructions**.

5. **Keep going!**

Cinq étapes vers la réussite

1. **Observez le chiffre supérieur de l'indication de mesure**. Frappez (dans les mains, chantez ou jouez sur une seule note) le rythme tout en maintenant une pulsation intérieure constante. Comptez mentalement au moins une mesure pour installer la pulsation avant de frapper le rythme ou de jouer la pièce.

2. **Repérez les motifs**. Tout en frappant le rythme, observez les contours de la mélodie, le mouvement et le style de la pièce caractérisé par les indications d'expression et par les nuances dynamiques.

3. **Observez les notes de basse**, leurs emplacements et leurs changements.

4. **Repérez les altérations accidentelles et autres directives**.

5. **Ne vous arrêtez pas !**

Fünf Schritte zum Erfolg

1. **Sieh dir die obere Zahl der Taktangabe an**. Schlage (klatsche, singe oder spiele eine Note) den Rhythmus, wobei du immer das Metrum spüren solltest. Zähle mindestens einen Takt im Kopf vor, bevor du zu spielen beginnst.

2. **Achte auch auf Muster**. Während du den Rhythmus schlägst, solltest du dir die melodische Form und den Stil des Stückes ansehen, der durch die Vortragsbezeichnungen und die dynamischen Angaben angegeben wird.

3. **Achte auf die Bassnoten** und beobachte, wo sie vorkommen und sich ändern.

4. **Achte auf alle zusätzlichen Vorzeichen und Anweisungen**.

5. **Spiele immer weiter!**

Performance directions used in this section:

Indications d'expression utilisées dans cette section :

Vortragsbezeichnungen, die in diesem Teil vorkommen:

Adagio	slowly	lent	langsam
Allegro	fast/quick	rapide, vif	schnell, lebhaft
Allegro moderato	moderately fast	modérément rapide	mäßig schnell
Andante	at a walking pace	allant	gehend
Andantino	a little quicker than andante	un peu plus vite qu'*andante*	etwas schneller als Andante
Con moto	with movement	avec mouvement	mit Bewegung
Crescendo (*cresc.*)	gradually getting louder	de plus en plus fort	allmählich lauter werdend
Leggiero	light	léger	leicht
Moderato	at a moderate speed	modéré	in gemäßigtem Tempo
Rall. (rallentando)	gradually getting slower	en ralentissant	allmählich langsamer werdend
Simile (*sim.*)	continue in the same way	de la même façon	auf gleiche Weise

Section 6 – Revision; keys of F major and D minor

Section 6 – Révision ; tonalités de *fa* majeur et de *ré* mineur

Teil 6 – Durchsicht; die Tonarten F-Dur und d-Moll

192.

193.

194.

195.

196.

197.

198.

199.

This piece begins on the fourth beat of the bar in 4-time. Count 1 2 3 before you begin.

Cette pièce débute sur le 4e temps d'une mesure à 4 temps. Comptez 1, 2, 3, avant de commencer.

Dieses Stück beginnt auf dem vierten Schlag in einem 4/4-Takt. Zähle 1 2 3 vor, bevor du anfängst.

200.

201.

202.

203.

204.

205.

206.

207.

This piece begins on the fourth
beat of the bar in 4-time.
Count 1 2 3 before you begin.

Cette pièce débute sur le 4e temps
d'une mesure à 4 temps.
Comptez 1, 2, 3, avant de commencer.

Dieses Stück beginnt auf dem
vierten Schlag in einem 4/4-Takt.
Zähle 1 2 3 vor, bevor du anfängst.

208.

209.

210.

211.

212.

213.

214.

215.

216.

217.

218.

219.

| This piece begins on the fourth beat of the bar in 4-time. Count 1 2 3 before you begin. | Cette pièce débute sur le 4e temps d'une mesure à 4 temps. Comptez 1, 2, 3, avant de commencer. | Dieses Stück beginnt auf dem vierten Schlag in einem 4/4-Takt. Zähle 1 2 3 vor, bevor du anfängst. |

220.

221.

222.

223.

224.

Andantino

225.

Con moto

226.

Allegro moderato

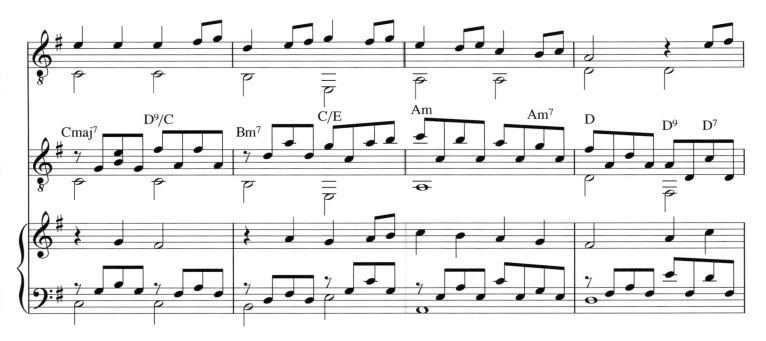

227.

228.

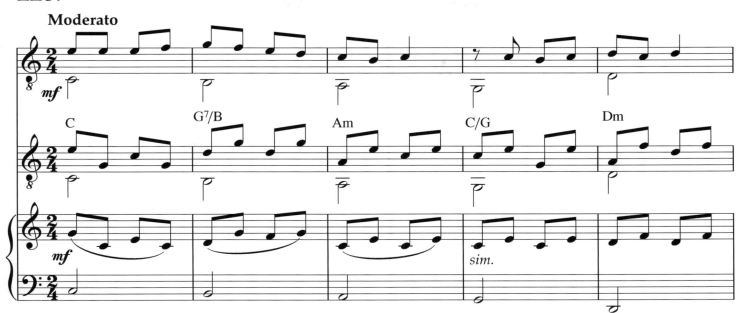

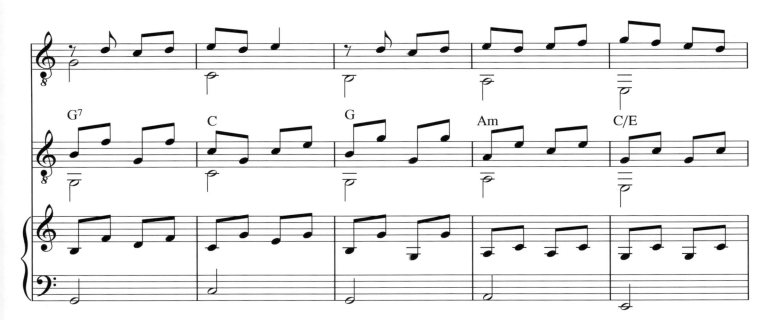

Glossary
Glossaire
Glossar

Note performance directions together with their translations used throughout the book so that you have a complete list. Writing them down will help you to remember them.

Inscrivez ici les indications d'exécution utilisées dans ce volume et leur traduction pour en établir une liste complète. Le fait de les noter vous aidera à les retenir.

Schreibe hier alle Vortragsangaben, die im Buch verwendet werden, zusammen mit ihren Übersetzungen auf, so dass du eine vollständige Liste hast. Das Aufschreiben wird dir dabei helfen sie einzuprägen.

Adagio	Slowly	Lent	Langsam